The King is Coming
Coming Alive at Advent

Jennifer Hand

Contents

Adventing

(P.S.: I think that is a word I made up)

I LIKE TO feel like we are sitting down and having a conversation at a coffee shop together. One of my favorite things is when people say they feel like they can hear my voice as they are reading something I have written.

Maybe that is why I like to use all of the descriptive-way-long-so-my-editor-isn't-sure-how-you-can-hyphenate-so-many words—because frankly, I like words.

(And this is why I never got my Friday treat in elementary school or get to go to recess for that matter, because I was always in trouble for NEVER not talking.)

When I set about writing a second Christmas book for you, I wanted to use all of the words.

It's funny. I sat down on so many hours , so many days, so many weeks and tried to type the words.

And those words would not come.

I wanted to offer <u>25 Days of Coming Alive at Christmas</u>: Volume Two. (Here is an excellent opportunity to insert a shameless plug for another book of mine, <u>25 Days to Coming Alive at Christmas,</u> available on Amazon at any time for you. P.S.: in case you have not noticed, I also really like adding long parentheses to things—making all the English fans among us shudder.)

Finally, after much prayer and weeks of trying to write THAT book, God gave me this book.

He wanted me to use a lot fewer words and give you time with Him and His word.

So here we go.

Welcome to our advent study.

I know you want the official definition of advent, don't you?

So I went to the very official source—Wikipedia. And I must say it had a pretty great definition, so I am going to include it here.

> *Advent is a season observed in many Christian churches as a time of expectant waiting and preparation for both the celebration of the Nativity of Jesus at Christmas and the return of Jesus at the Second Coming. The term is a version of the Latin word meaning "coming."*

I love these words — expectant waiting. Because let's be honest, waiting comes with some hard connotations. I do not love waiting.

But *expectant* waiting. That seems to have a different weight to it.

Waiting. Watching and preparing my heart. For what?

For the coming of the King. That's what Christmas is all about. The King of Glory broke brought the light of heaven to the darkness of the earth.

Emmanuel. He came and dwelt among us.

I want to celebrate His coming. I want to celebrate that the King *has* come, but I also want to watch for how He *is* coming, how He is showing up in my life daily.

Emmanuel is still God with me. With you.

So here we are. Together. Adventing. (I really think I made that verb up. Or at the very least, spell check didn't seem to like it.)

I remember loving Advent as a child. I remember our pastor standing around the advent wreath and each week lighting the candle for the week. Occasionally, they would have families come up and light the candle of the week.

I always wanted to be that one. I wanted to be the one who was able to light the candle. I think the pastor must have known that I have been known to burn things down.

Like the only outhouse in a remote village.

Our the backdrop of a stage where I was speaking.

Or catching my dress on fire as a bridesmaid in a wedding and having to put the fire out with baptismal water.

(These are all true stories friends!)

So, I never got to be the one to light the candle of the Advent wreath. But I still remember those moments.

Each week the candle represents something.

We are going to advent together. Feel free to light a candle, but only if you can do so responsibly, unlike me.

At the beginning of each of the four weeks of advent, there will be a chapter for you to read. Together we will look at the theme of that week.

We will wait with the prophets in the expectation of the coming king.

We will watch with Mary and Joseph the kingdom coming.

We will worship the king who has come.

And we will be filled with wonder at the glory in this story. (Do you see the alliteration I did there?)

We will have scripture for you to read each day. I am deliberately choosing shorter passages of scripture so you can rest and linger in the words instead of rushing through.

That's where I want God's words to speak to you. I love that the Bible is living and active and God speaks. He is longing to speak to you, and He will meet you.

So grab your favorite Bible or Bible app. I mean, the Bible app will read to you in a British accent if you want. Technology these days.

Take a minute out of the holiday hustle and bustle each day and watch for the King.

As you read the scriptures for each day, I encourage you to ask these questions:

What do I learn about God in these scriptures?
How does what I learned about God change me?
How am I experiencing the King
who has come, God with us?

Sometimes, we speed through things. Or we overcomplicate them. (Or maybe that is just me.)

I want this to be an Advent where we slow down together. Meditate on scripture in a new way. Lean in. Listen.

Wait. Watch. Worship in wonder at the King who has come and is coming again.

x

ADVENTING WEEK ONE
Wait

A Big Welcome to You–
You are Invited to the Table

*T*HERE ARE SO many things I love about the holidays. I am your typical cheesy "love all the traditions, the sights, the sounds, the smells of Christmas" girl.

Give me a pine with a twinge of snow-scented candlelit night, while sipping mugs of spiced apple cider around a Christmas tree with friends wearing an ugly Christmas sweater (of course) getting ready for the tacky Christmas gift exchange and I am one happy girl.

(Too much Hallmark Christmas movie watching perhaps as I paint that picture, huh?) The only thing missing is a snow globe, Christmas tree farm, and spilling my coffee on an unsuspecting person that happens to be walking down our small-town street because he has come to take over the family-owned cookie factory and he becomes my future husband.

It's currently the end of September, and even typing those sentences above brought such happy feelings.

Granted, it has been a crazy hot summer, and it is still 96 degrees here, so I had to turn on the Christmas music and lower the air conditioning to feel the Christmas cheer.

One of my favorite things about Christmas is the parties. The gatherings. The party food. Although my unfortunate late in life allergy developments means no more sausage balls or yummy melt in your mouth creamy dips—can we all take a moment to mourn for me?

When I take a personality test, they all show up with the same results across the board. I love to be where the party is, but I am not very good at remembering details, like sending in my RSVP.

I love the laughter that comes with friends and family around the table. A meal where all the food is running together on your plate and you almost choke on your chicken because you are laughing so hard at your friend telling a story.

There was that one time my friend did choke on chicken. Having to do the Heimlich maneuver did spoil the moment.

Currently, I have the "family table" from my childhood in my little one-bedroom apartment. This table was the source of so many fun memories growing up. My mom is an amazing cook, and dinners were always a fun experience at our house. There was always room for more at the table, and let's be honest, I only had friends in high school because they all wanted to come over and eat my mom's hashbrown casserole.

Why do I say all of this? Because I want to invite you to the table. To gather around. To take a deep breath, and maybe smell the pine-scented candle while you are at it, if you like that sort of thing.

Grab your favorite warm beverage (mine is strong sludge of black coffee of course), and feel free to wear your Christmas pajamas.

Let's be honest. In the chaos of Christmas, it is very easy to miss the Christ of Christmas. To forget that Jesus left the holy of heaven to walk in the dust of the earth for us.

The prophets of the Old Testament promised us He would come, and He did. The long-anticipated Messiah.

Jesus coming to our rescue is the greatest gift. He came to rescue us from our sin, our selves and to provide His presence in our present circumstances.

Jesus is one great gift: Emmanuel, God with us.

There are many characters in the Christmas story. Mary, Joseph, shepherds, wise men, we have seen them all in the nativity scenes usually gathered around the central figure in the story—Jesus.

We cannot forget these were real people just like you and me. People who had been waiting for a rescuer. For a Messiah. These Christmas characters were some who God chose to reveal His glory and show Himself in their stories.

Often in unexpected plans and places.

A field with sheep? A stinky stable for animals? A virgin's womb?

And fear not. Maybe you are new to this whole thing. Maybe you don't know the characters of Christmas well? Maybe you only know snatches of the story.

This is the party for you. That's what is fun about a Christmas party. You could enter as strangers and leave as friends. I mean, who wouldn't be friends after you make fun of the random Jell-o mold, eat yummy Christmas fudge, and fight over who wins the favorite gift in the white elephant gift exchange? How couldn't you know each other better than when you came?

I am still slightly bitter about a coffee cup that I had in my pretty little hands one year until the person who had drawn the number 1 got the last pick and took it away.

My party-loving self pictures us sitting around a long dinner table, lingering—not in the typical Christmas rush.

We are sitting at the table, but so are the characters of Christmas. Mary is seated to your left, Joseph beside her, of course. The Shepherds feel a bit uncomfortable sitting, so they tend to keep getting up to look into the backyard like they are missing some sheep or something.

Elizabeth and Zechariah are there recounting the birth of Jesus' cousin.

And at the center of the table is Jesus. After all, He is the one who invited us to the table.

Who is that again?

We all have those moments when we see someone at a party that we know who we are maybe supposed to know, but we cannot place them. So many things can run through our minds at that moment.

Did I go to school with them? Or was it them who ran the vegetable stand at the farmers' market that I went to that one time. (Ok, I am going to be real honest right now. I have no idea where I got that sentence. I guess I am trying to be relevant here. I mean, we are in the farm-to-table days. #trendyJenn)

Let me be real with you. It gets even more complicated when you have a twin. In case you are unaware, I have an identical twin sister—which is the BEST until it's getting difficult in a conversation when you are not sure if you are supposed to know this person that you cannot quite place or if they think you are your twin sister.

Things get dicey when they start asking how your husband is. My sister is married and has four kids, and I am single. I usually play along even when they think I am Michelle until the question comes up, how is your husband? I tell them I don't know where he is (because, well, that's the truth) and they don't quite know what to say from there.

Don't worry. I do tell those that are confused that I am not Michelle.

Then there are the family reunion moments. That long-lost relative comes up and pinches your cheeks, tells you they have known you since you were crawling, and they are so excited to see you— and you have NO idea who they are. Then they asked the dreaded, "Do you remember me?"

You are frantically trying to make eye contact with your mom for her to mouth, "This is Jean, your third cousin by marriage. Don't you remember she is married to Mark who belongs to your great-great aunt Betsy?"

(P.S.: if you are in my family and reading this, don't try to place those names. They are made up.)

Of course, I remember you, Jean. How are Mark and Aunt Betsy?

As I mentioned before, I want this book to feel like we are sitting around the dinner table at a Christmas party with the characters of Christmas. I want the stories that can sometimes become familiar to change us all over again as we think in new ways about the powerful truth that the people involved in the Christmas story in the Bible were real.

They had real, ordinary lives that were changed forever by an extraordinary miracle.

The perfect son of God leaving the streets of heaven to enter the earth. To enter our broken world so that one day, His body would be broken on a cross to fix our broken lives.

This rescue story was not a surprise, random idea. A rescue plan was put into place by God the minute sin entered the world through Adam and Eve. A Messiah. A Redeemer.

I am inviting the prophets to join us at the table at the Christmas party because they had a part in the Christmas story. They were proclaiming the promises that He was coming. The rescuer that had been awaited since Adam and Eve would come.

Heaven would burst forth onto the earth. It would require waiting. And in the waiting, God was working.

The Promise Maker is the Promise Keeper.

Let's pull up a chair next to the prophet Isaiah. Here is a little-known fact that I have never heard a preacher sneak into his sermon. Did you know that the prophet Isaiah walked around barefoot and naked for THREE years?

> *"Then the Lord said, "As my servant Isaiah has walked naked and barefoot for three years as a sign." (Isaiah 20:3)*

Talk about radical obedience to the calling of God. I am grateful the Lord has never asked me to walk barefoot and naked to get the point across. There was the one time I tripped walking up the stairs to a stage because I was trying to be all fancy and wear high heels and may or may not have mooned the whole crowd I was about to speak to—but it did not last three years, for goodness' sakes.

Since we invited Isaiah to the Christmas party, I made sure to include the reminder that clothing was **not** optional in the invitation, but that your tacky Christmas sweater was.

> *"Therefore, the Lord Himself will give you a sign. Behold the virgin hall conceive and bear a son, and He shall call his name Immanuel." (Isaiah 7:14)*

A promise proclaimed by a prophet. A virgin birth will result in a son called Immanuel. The translation of Immanuel is worth getting excited. Let out a little "glory" if you want to. This little word in this big promise has life-changing meaning for us.

God with us.

*"In the beginning was the Word and the Word was with God, and the Word was God. He was in the beginning with God. All things were made through him, and without him was not any thing made that was made. In Him was life, and the life was the light of men. **And the Word became flesh** and dwelt among us, and we have seen his glory, glory as of the only Son from the Father, full of grace and truth." (John 1:1-4, 14)*

This is good stuff, friends. Isaiah prophesied that God would come and walk among us. And He did. Through Jesus, the Word became flesh.

Truthfully, it sounds like a fairy tale. The ultimate rescue story as the Creator comes from heaven to be with those He created.

This is the glory of Christmas, truly what changes everything.

God. With. You!

He is with you in the chaos of your Christmas season. He is with you on the mundane Monday and in the "I am not sure I can make it until Friday" moments.

He is with you when you fill full of life and joy. When you are enjoying watching yet another Hallmark Christmas movie in your pajamas sipping hot cocoa. (So maybe that is what I want to be doing right now.)

I am praying for you as I type these words. What do you have going on in your life? As I pray, I sense some are confused, searching for direction. Some have a longing for more—more intimacy with the Christ of Christmas.

I sense some of you are in what feels like the battle of your life. A relational battle, a battle to believe God is faithful, and He does see you. A bank account battle. A dreading going to work each day battle.

A what is going to happen in this family situation battle.

And then some feel bored. Bored with life, bored with your relationship with God, bored with your relationship with others.

And those who are busy and trying to juggle it all.

Immanuel. God. With. You.

He is with you as you face this Christmas season. He is with you as you look at your calendar (or maybe you are like me and wondering where you put that calendar this time?) and feel overwhelmed by it all.

He is with you when you cannot imagine how that family gathering will go this year.

We invited Isaiah to the Christmas party dinner table because He was a signal to the Old Testament world that the New Testament Jesus was coming. If you read the book of Isaiah, you will see that the people needed a signal, a promise of hope coming.

They needed to know in the dark that there would be light.

There is something about darkness that does make you appreciate the light so much more.

Recently our church had a church-wide campout. The kind where you pull out good old fashioned tents and sleep on the ground without electricity. It's funny. People were all in for the idea until they weren't—when it was going to be around ninety degrees (in October!!).

(True confession - I camped with them during the day and went home to a bed at night, so I cannot say anything).

Tennessee had been experiencing quite a long drought. Do you want to know how to cure a drought? Plan a church-wide tent camping trip.

You know that feeling when a storm is brewing. You can feel it in the atmosphere. The wind changes and picks up. The clouds begin to form. And if you are tent camping in the wilderness, you start looking at all the fancy weather apps on your phone to try to see how bad the storm will be and how near it will get.

If you are my sister, you start to obsessively asking around if anyone is getting reception because my sister does not remain so calm in the event of a storm.

I left for the evening right before the storm broke. But I could picture my sister frantically pulling her family to shelter in the minivan once the first rumble of thunder occurred. The storm did pick up, and even I had to seek shelter because I could not see to drive. I did not make it that far out of the wilderness boondocks where we were camping, so I ended up sheltering in what I think was the cross between a gas station and a flea market.

The flea market tents were flying everywhere, and I was not sure if I should stay inside my car or risk the lightning strikes to grab those tents protecting the flea market wares.

I decided to choose my life versus the tents full of knock-off trinkets, so I stayed in my car.

I was so tickled the next day when I arrived back at camp. There had been some marital disputes in the middle of the night when it started to storm again.

The wives of the group wanted to grab all of their families from the tents and jump in their minivans to sleep among the car seats, along with the "forgot to throw away" juice boxes and sticky leftover donuts crammed in the back seat.

My friends' husbands were not sure they wanted to find a shelter in the storm other than the tent. They were none too thrilled when their wives insisted they needed to get up and take shelter from this storm.

What in the world does this have to do with Christmas, you might be asking? (Well, I would be if I were you.)

Some of the Israelites in the day of Isaiah needed someone to point out that they were in a storm. They had turned away from worshiping God to worshiping the idols of their day, and it seemed okay to them. Isaiah was like the poor lone weatherman telling them of the approaching storm.

They needed to repent and return.

He was not just the weatherman warning them of the storm. He was also like those poor weathermen who stand outside in hurricanes barely able to hold on to their microphones because the winds are so strong. The weathermen who tell you not only to seek shelter immediately but where to find the safest place to find shelter.

Isaiah was calling out to those in darkness and reminding them of the light. He was also sharing the promise of the Messiah, who was to come.

The One we celebrate this Christmas season.

Listen in with me to his report. Lean in like you would if you were watching the Weather Channel during a storm. You can even picture Isaiah trying to hold on to his microphone.

> *"The people who walked in darkness have seen a great light; those who dwell in a land of deep darkness on them has light shined. For to us, a child is born, to us, a son is given; and the government shall be upon His shoulder, and his name shall be called Wonderful Counselor, Mighty God, Everlasting Father Prince of Peace. Of the increase of his government and of peace, there will be no end on the throne of David and his kingdom."*
> (Isaiah 9:1, 6-7)

He is giving the people a promise of shelter from the storm.

The promise of a child born who would change everything. There are storms all around today. Just look at social media or the news. You do not have to listen or scroll long to see that.

There are storms in your own heart and life. Relationship issues. Job issues. Doubts. Fears. Sickness. Death. Grief. Hurt. Misunderstandings.

Whew, that last paragraph sure did lower the mood, huh?

Here is joy. Isaiah 9 has happened. Unto us a child was born. The son of God has come. He is our Wonderful Counselor.

He is your mighty God. He is your Everlasting Father. He is the Prince of Peace.

Heaven knows we all need some peace.

We do not have to celebrate the gift of Jesus only at Christmastime, but it is a special time. A time where we set out the nativity scenes with Jesus in the manger at the center.

Unless you cannot find your baby Jesus, so you draw a face on a cotton ball instead. (Speaking for a friend here, of course.)

Where have you been trying to run to shelter lately? Are you staying in a tent because you do not want to get up from where you are? A tent that when the storms blow can get taken away by the wind?

Or are you finding shelter in the One who is our safe place? I know I can easily try to find shelter in people, places, or things instead of the stable that held the gift of the baby Jesus.

Welcome another guest-- Micah

Micah. This is a book of the Bible that does not get talked about very often. It's tiny and hidden in there in the Minor Prophet section of the Old Testament.

Let's be honest here. It's not very often that we find ourselves saying, "I really would like to take a deep dive into the Minor Prophets."

These small books do have some amazing big truths packed in them.

Micah was a prophet around the same time as Isaiah. He and Isaiah would probably be hanging around in the same corner of the Christmas party drinking eggnog and talking about their good ol' days as prophets.

(Side note: That has nothing to do with anything spiritual, but I could not help giggling as I typed out the word eggnog. I remembered the time my cousins spiked the eggnog, and my very conservative and classy grandmother just kept going back for more until she had a LITTLE too much "eggnog.")

Like Isaiah, Micah brought some good news and some bad news. He started with a whole lot of bad news. The title of chapter 1 in Micah in my

ESV Study Bible is "The Coming Destruction." There are lots of woes pronounced to the people, warnings of judgment.

But then there is a turn in Micah 5.

> *"But you, O Bethlehem Ephrathat, who are too little to be among the clans of Judah, from you shall come forth for me one who is to be ruler of Israel, whose origin is from old, from ancient days. Therefore he shall give them up until the time when she who is in labor has given birth; then the rest of his brothers shall return to the people of Israel. And he shall stand and shepherd his flock in the strength of the Lord, in the majesty of the name of the Lord his God. **And they shall dwell secure, for now, He shall be great to the ends of the earth. And He shall be their peace.**" (Micah 5:2-5)*

Tucked in this little book through the mouth of a little prophet named Micah is a life-changing promise. (Truthfully, I have no idea if he was little; it just seemed to work there for dramatic effect.)

From Bethlehem will come one from ancient of days who will shepherd his people, who will be great and **who will be their peace.**

This was prophesied way before Jesus burst from heaven to earth in the form of an infant who cried and needed his diaper changed.

This was a promise with detail in it. This Messiah would be born in Bethlehem. Little Bethlehem. I love that God chose a place that no one noticed. A place that would seem to be the last place for heaven to burst forth onto earth.

Micah 5:2 tells us that Bethlehem was too little to be among the tribes of Judah. I love that God chose the little town of Bethlehem to bring big change to the world. A place that would change everything.

Maybe you feel that way sometimes. Like someone that is overlooked or too small or insignificant to matter. I love that we have a God who chooses the unnoticed and looked over.

He sees you and knows you and is going to shine His glory through you.

Judges 6 tells us about Gideon. Just for kicks, let's go ahead and invite him to our Christmas party. He can hang out with Micah and Isaiah in the Old Testament corner of the room. He was around in a difficult time for the Israelites. The Midianites were attacking the Israelites.

> *"...and the hand of Midian overpowered Israel, and because of Midian, the people of Israel made for themselves the dens that are in the mountains and the caves and the strongholds." (Judges 6:2)*

The people were in hiding in strongholds to try and find safety.

(Does this remind you of what we talked about on Day 2 and where we run to for shelter? If it doesn't, just don't tell me because I want to be able to give you your gold star for being a great student!)

Gideon was hiding in the wine press when we find him encountering an angel of the Lord.

> *"And the angel of the Lord appeared to him and said to him, 'The Lord is with you, O mighty man of valor.' And Gideon said to him, 'Please sir, if the Lord is with us, why has all of this happened to us?' And the Lord turned to him and said, 'Go in this might of yours and save Israel from the hand of Midian, do not I send you? ' And He said to him, 'Please Lord, how can I save Israel? **Behold my clan is the weakest in Manasseh, and I am the least in my Father's house.'"** (Judges 6:12-15)*

Gideon: The weakest clan and the smallest in his house.

Bethlehem: The smallest, too little to be among the tribe of Judah.

Yet God called Gideon a mighty warrior.

God placed in Bethlehem the birth of the mightiest warrior.

> *And Joseph also went up from Galilee, from the town of Nazareth to Judea, to the city of David, which is called Bethlehem, because he was of the house and lineage of David, to be registered with Mary, his betrothed, who was with child. And while they were there, the time came for her to give birth. And she gave birth to her firstborn son and wrapped him in swaddling clothes and laid him in a manger because there was no place for them in the inn. (Luke 2:4-7)*

Imagine what God wants to do in and through you for his glory story. The enemy loves to tell us all the reasons we deserve to be overlooked for the kingdom of God—but when we accept the invitation to know Jesus, we carry the presence and power of Jesus.

You carry the power and presence of Jesus.

Honestly, I could keep going on about this cool prophecy tucked into the book about Jesus being born in Bethlehem. How this is a reminder to us that God is into details, and He is a promise keeper.

The God who detailed the Christmas story is detailing your life.

God, who makes promises, keeps promises.

The God who took the little and did much—He is working His glory in your story.

The Jesus Genes

In a previous book of mine, I made a true confession, which I am going to add in this book again.

In college, my sister and I had the same major (human services in case you were dying to know), so we took a lot of classes together.

We both tend to be—shall I say, the procrastinator types. (Don't ask me how many days I have until the deadline of this book because I don't want you to know how much I procrastinate!)

We were tasked with the assignment to do a genogram. In case you are not familiar with that word, this is a complex drawing of your family tree that shows the lineage of your family plus other bonus tidbits, such as addiction patterns, divorce, family triangulation and more. (Listen, you have no need to know what that means unless you are getting your Masters in counseling right now, so no worries.)

My sister and I waited until the last minute, and I remember quite well us staying up until the wee hours of the morning drawing this genogram on giant poster board paper in the lobby of the girls' dorm, fueled by Ramen noodles and brownies, of course.

Here is the deal. There have been lots of divorces, remarriages, and such in our family among our cousins. So once it got late enough, we may or may not have started just making stuff up.

However, for some crazy reason, we did not collaborate. When we turned that project in, our professor wisely wanted to know why identical twins had differing family trees!

The Christmas story involves a complex family tree. It's interesting because the gospel of Matthew starts with a list of the whole thing.

Let's be honest here. I don't know about you, but when I see a long list of names in the Bible, it can be easy for me to want to tune out and skip over. Long lists of names also mean that I for one do not want to be the one to volunteer to read out loud that passage in church.

When you dig into it, the opening line of Matthew 1 packs a much more exciting punch than it may seem at first glance.

"The book of the genealogy of Jesus Christ, the Son of David, the Son of Abraham."

If it were a movie, it might seem like a strange way to start. If it were a Hallmark Christmas movie, it would more than likely start out with the scene of a big town executive forced to visit the small town Kristmas Kringle cookie factory instead of using the word genealogy.

For the Jewish audience at the time, this was a huge opening line. To the Jewish people, family lineage was a big deal. They knew of the promises given to their ancestors from what family line Jesus would come

In Genesis 22:18, Abraham receives a promise that in his offspring all the nations of the earth would be blessed. The promise was a covenant promise that God was making with Abraham. A promise of His unfolding plan.

God also made a promise to David.

> *"When your days are fulfilled and you lie down with your fathers, I will raise up your offspring after you, who shall come from your body, and I will establish his kingdom." (2 Sam 7:11)*

If we had more time and space, we could take a deep dive into this covenant promise and all the different times throughout the Old Testament that this covenant made with David was brought up. It was a big deal.

God highlighted it throughout because He had a plan. A family line plan that would ultimately lead to the one who would rescue us.

A line that traced from the promise made to Father Abraham (Are you finding yourself like me wanting to shout out a hearty had many sons when you read his name?) and to David, to a baby born in Bethlehem named Jesus, to you and me.

Maybe you, like me need, a reminder again that the Promise Maker is the Promise Keeper.

David would be a fun one to have at the Christmas party dinner. If I had drawn his name for the five dollar gift exchange, I would have probably bought him a slingshot. After all, he seems to know what to do with one.

One slingshot and a few stones= giant down. (2 Samuel 21)

When the hour got later and the conversation got more serious, maybe he would talk about how he had found a God of forgiveness when he committed adultery with Bathsheba and then murdered her husband. After all, that is not light appetizer, pass the sausage balls conversation.

I wonder how I would respond if God gave me a big promise like He gave David in 2 Samuel 7 — let me in on His plan to establish His kingdom through my family line.

Let's take a peek into David's response. It seems like he had a "Who am I?" type moment, as I imagine I would as well.

> *"Then King David went in and sat before the Lord AND SAID, 'WHO AM I, O LORD GOD, AND WHAT IS MY HOUSE, THAT YOU HAVE BROUGHT ME THUS FAR? And yet this was a small thing in your eyes, O Lord GOD. YOU HAVE SPOKEN ALSO OF YOUR SERVANT'S HOUSE FOR A GREAT WHILE TO COME, AND THIS IS INSTRUCTION FOR MANKIND, O LORD GOD! And what more can David say to you? For you know your servant, O Lord GOD! Because of your promise, and according to your own heart, you have brought about all this greatness, to make your servant know it.'" (2 Samuel 7:18-22)*

I bet you have had your "Who am I?" moments also. God's promises to us can seem too big for our small selves.

Just like God knew David, He knows you and me. It's because of His promises and the heart of who He is that He does great "more than we can ask or imagine" things.

Christmas is very close to the new year. What if, during this Christmas season, you take some time to pause and pray for what the BIG God is doing in your life through what sometimes seems small?

God chose to use David and bring the Messiah through his family line.

He is choosing to use you, and you get to carry on the family tree of Jesus.

Week One Reading Guide

Day 1: Isaiah 7:14

Day 2: John 1

Day 3: Isaiah 9:1-7

Day 4: Psalm 91

Day 5: Micah 5:2-4

Day 6: Judges 6:11-25

Day 7: Matthew 1

What do I learn about God in these scriptures?

How does what I learned about God change me?

How am I experiencing the King who has come, God with us?

ADVENTING WEEK TWO
Watch and Hope

"**O** LITTLE TOWN OF Bethlehem how still we see thee lie!"

I love a good Christmas carol line just like this one from "O Little Town of Bethlehem."

Can I say, however, that I do feel like all Christmas carols tend to be sung in octaves way too high for me to be able to sing along?

Bethlehem, the tiny town where heaven would come to earth and appear in the form of a baby. This baby, Jesus, would grow into a man. In John 6:34, Jesus gave a powerful statement.

> *"I am the bread of life; whoever comes to me shall not hunger, and whoever believes in me shall never thirst."*

Did you know that Bethlehem means t*he house of bread*? How amazing is that little detail? The one who calls Himself the bread of life was born in a city called *the house of bread.*

We are going to invite some ladies to our Christmas party dinner that probably are the ones tending the bread to make sure it doesn't burn.

Don't you hate it when that is your job? I am THE WORST if you tell me to watch the biscuits or the garlic bread while the butter is melting to make sure it does not burn. I will get distracted, and pretty soon, you will see smoke coming out of the oven and the garlic bread burnt to a crisp.

Let's talk with Ruth and Naomi at our Christmas party. They are there because they make the family tree of Jesus in Matthew 1.

Ruth is the mother of Obed, and Obed was the father of Jesse, and Jesse was the father of David— as in King David.

The House of Bread

Raise your hand with me if you like bread? Maybe like is not a strong enough word for you? My mouth waters thinking about nice hot, warm fresh bread—bonus points if it is homemade and slathered in good fancy butter.

I always have dreams of myself as a famous Food Network Star who makes the homemade bread, kneading the dough perfectly, placing it in the beautiful loaf pan, and it rising to be something a food blogger would want as a picture.

Instead, it usually turns out more like flour all over every crack in my kitchen (how exactly did the flour make its way onto the ceiling?), all over my face, and dough that will not rise.

Hard pancake-like bread, anyone?

There was a day when Bethlehem, the house of bread, was not living up to its name. There was no bread to be found because there was a famine in the land.

"In those days, when the judges ruled there was a famine in the land, and a man of Bethlehem in Judah went to sojourn in the country of Moab, he and his wife and his town sons." (Ruth 1:1)

This man's wife was Naomi, and his two sons were Mahlon and Chilion. (I wonder if they called him Chili for short?) They left "the house of bread" to try to find some bread.

The story could potentially be made into a Hallmark Christmas movie from there, except there is a little too much sadness for Hallmark. Maybe more a Netflix movie special?

Naomi's husband dies. Her sons take Moabite wives. Then the sons die. Naomi is left as a stranger in a foreign land and decides she needs to return to her home in Bethlehem.

In a plot twist, her one loyal daughter in law, Ruth, is determined to go back with Naomi. Ruth is making a pretty brave move considering Naomi was a grieving, bitter widow. She may not have been the most pleasant to go with on a long journey.

In Hallmark movies, the big city executive finds herself traveling to an unknown small town named Evergreen to save the fledgling cookie business Krinkles. Often, she is moving from New York to a small ski lodge covered in snow in remote Alaska, and her high heels do not seem to be working for her as she tries to navigate deep snowbanks.

Or at least that is the plot of the movie I fell asleep watching last night.

This time Ruth was the one going to the foreign land.

> *But Ruth said, "Do not urge me to leave you or to return from following you. For where you go I will go, and where you lodge, I will lodge. Your people shall be my people, and your God my God." (Ruth 1:15)*

I imagine that Ruth had no idea that returning with her mother-in-law to Bethlehem, the city of bread, would land her in the Christmas story genealogy of Jesus in Matthew 1.

Do you need a reminder today that God is always guiding you? He is working His glory in your story.

He guided Ruth with Naomi to a land she did not know. And *she just so happened* to come to a field belonging to Boaz when she went out searching for wheat to make bread.

Ruth was looking for the beginnings of bread.

God was going to use this search for bread to connect Ruth and Boaz, who one day would be in the lineage of Jesus, the Bread of Life.

God is in the details.

Sometimes we have to step into the unfamiliar and wonder where provision will come to see Him give us our *just so happened* plot twists. In these moments, we get to watch in hope for God.

Boaz took good care of Ruth that day. *It just so happens* that Boaz was a kinsman of Naomi's, which made him a kinsman-redeemer. He could take Ruth as his wife and redeem the family line of Naomi.

> *"So Boaz took Ruth, and she became his wife. And he went in to her, and the Lord gave her conception, and she bore a son. Then the women said to Naomi, 'Blessed be the Lord **who has not left you** this day without a redeemer and may his name be renowned in Israel. He shall be to you a restorer of life and a nourisher of your old age, for your daughter-in-law who loves you, who is more to you than seven sons has given birth to him.' Then Naomi took the child and laid him on her lap and became his nurse. And the women of the neighborhood gave him a name, saying, 'A Son has been born to Naomi.' They named him Obed. **He was the father of Jesse, the father of David.** (Ruth 4:13-17)*

Naomi and her first husband left Bethlehem, the house of bread, because of a lack of bread.

Naomi returned with Ruth and found herself in the field of Boaz, the provision of bread.

Jesus, the Bread of Life, started His life in Bethlehem, the city of bread.

Because the Bread of Life was broken for us, we can find life.

I love the reminder today that God orchestrates the *"just so happened"* moments in our lives.

He is directing you. He will provide for you. He is a kinsman-redeemer for you, and He is the broken bread of life for YOU. That is a Christmas story worth celebrating.

Boaz was the redeemer for Ruth in Bethlehem.

Jesus was born in Bethlehem to be our Redeemer.

Hope

Have you ever watched in hope for something to happen in your life for long periods?

Sometimes for so long that you no longer can attach the word hope to your watching?

It is hard to hold hope and longing in the waiting.

It's time for me to introduce you to Elizabeth and Zechariah. You will find them playing games in the family room. Zechariah is killing it at charades because well, as you will find out, he was only able to communicate through charades for a while.

Elizabeth and Zechariah were a favorite couple of many. They played auntie and uncle to a lot of their friends' kids because they did not have any children of their own.

Elizabeth was heavily involved in women's ministry at their local church. Zechariah was on the church staff. Both of them faithfully spent their time serving God.

They knew God. They loved God.

They worshiped God.

But I imagined there were parts of their hearts that struggled to put their hope in God.

Waiting can do that. Unfilled longings, unanswered prayers, things happening in a time much slower than we imagined—this is enough to cause some complications in holding hope.

We meet Elizabeth and Zechariah in Luke 1. You may be very familiar with their stories in the Bible. Sometimes, however, we become so familiar that we forget to put their stories in real life.

Picture your single cousin at the family reunion when all the great aunts gather around her and hound her with the "why are you not married yet?" questions. Picture your cousin trying to sneak away in her embarrassment and hide among the children sitting at the kids' table.

Picture your friend that is desperate to have a baby. Who has waited time after time for that positive pregnancy test. Imagine what she feels like at the party when she is holding her best friend's baby.

A desire to continue to hold onto hope while holding a baby in her arms who is not hers.

We all have an unmet longings or unanswered prayers of some sort in our lives. Something we are waiting on. Elizabeth and Zechariah's just happened to be very visible to the people.

"In the days of Herod, king of Judea, there was a priest named Zechariah, of the division of Abijah. And he had a wife from the daughters of Aaron, and her name was Elizabeth. And they were both righteous before God, walking blameless in all the commandments and statutes of the Lord. But they had no child because Elizabeth was barren, and both were advanced in years." (Luke 1:5-7)

In the times Elizabeth and Zechariah were living, being barren would have brought shame. Having children was your identity.

Imagine the years of trying to hold onto hope in this barren place.

I want to pause right here.

This is where we go from small talk at a party to diving into the real stuff.

What is your barren place? Have you given up hope in this barren place? What would it look like for you to invite God's light into your barren place?

I am going to pause and do that right now. Would you join me?

Will you muster up some bravery and hold your hands open in hope before the Lord?

Will you tell Him again what you are hoping to see? What are you scared to talk to God about in your prayers?

Open hands and open hearts. I am joining you here, friend.

Surprised by God

The longer we wait the easier it is to forget to watch for God's miracles.

Zechariah was doing his regular priestly duties when God showed up even when he was not watching for Him.

He was worshiping as part of his priestly duties, burning the incense in the temple that day. However, I do not think he was watching for God to come with an answer to his prayer.

> *"And the whole multitude of the people were praying outside at the hour of incense. And there appeared to him an angel of the Lord standing on the right side of the altar of incense."*

Surprise! It always tends to take someone by surprise when an angel shows up. That sometimes happens in Hallmark movies as well.

"And Zechariah was troubled when he saw him and fear fell upon him. But the angel said to Him, " Do not be afraid, Zechariah, for your prayer has been heard, and your wife Elizabeth will bear you a son, and you shall call his name John. And you will have joy and gladness, and many will rejoice at his birth, for he will be great before the Lord." (Luke 1:8-14)

This is exciting stuff here! Exclamation point worthy!

#unexpected #surprise #hopeinbarrenplaces

I am not sure how I would respond in this situation. An angel shows up and tells me I am going to get what I had probably given up hope on.

Hope in the impossible may not feel so possible.

How did Zechariah respond?

> *"And Zechariah said to the angel, 'How shall I know this? For I am an old man, and my wife is advanced in years.' And the angel answered him, 'I am Gabriel, who stands in the presence of God, and I was sent to speak to you and to bring you this good news. And behold, you will be silent and unable to speak until the day that these things take place because you did not believe my words which be fulfilled in their time.'"*

Do you remember that old show *Touched by an Angel?* Here we have a special edition of *Silenced by an Angel.*

(Okay, so I realize that was a cheesy pun, but I did crack myself up there, so thank you for humoring me.)

This is why Zechariah is GREAT to be on a team with in charades at our party.

After Zechariah comes out from the temple, he kept making signs to them while remaining mute.

God had shown up in the barren space.

"After these days his wife Elizabeth conceived, and for five months she kept herself hidden saying, 'Thus the Lord has done for me in the days when he looked on me, to take away my reproach among the people.'" (Luke 1:24)

This Christmas, let's watch in hope for the unexpected. Big and small. Surprises from God. Holding onto hope. Watching in hope. Responding in hope.

"The Spiritual Ones"

It can be so easy to categorize people. To compare ourselves to them.

One category I can catch myself putting people in is "those are the spiritual ones." I can see a certain person and assume they probably never sin, are always humming a nice worship tune as they wash their dishes, and never speed when they are driving because they are never running late, of course.

I can compare my spiritualness (again, that is a made up Jenn word, but go with me) with theirs.

I think of monks who live in a monastery contemplating Jesus-y things all the time.

I went to a monastery on vacation once. My sister and a friend and I did not have money for a real vacation, so we found out you can take a "spiritual" vacation for a donation at a monastery.

We chose a beautiful one in South Carolina near Charleston and went. We decided we would follow the monk's schedule and vows of silence during the day—spending the day praying and contemplating and reading the Bible and then play cards in our cabin together in the evenings.

It was the most fun.

The strangest thing was eating our meals in silence. Who knew that a fork hitting a plate could be so loud. And that it would be possible to not choke on your food because you are trying so hard not to laugh at your sister who is making faces across the table from you.

My favorite time was when we joined the "brothers" in their morning and evening prayers as they sang beautifully through the Psalms. We were late the first night, and I did not know as we exited the darkly lit room to go to our room after the service that they would bless us with a slight splash of holy water on our head.

This was a surprise to me—and I was a surprise to them when I let out a scream, and the poor monks had to keep their vows of silence without laughing.

I laughed enough for them.

Does this knock me out of the "spiritual ones" category?

After the birth of Jesus, we meet some characters that I would call the "spiritual ones." They would be the ones probably asked to do the prayer over dinner.

Simeon is our first friend. Let's join him in Luke 2 at the temple.

*"And when the time came for their purification, according to the law of Moses, they brought him up to Jerusalem to present him to the Lord (as it is written in the Law of the Lord, 'Every male who first opens the womb shall be called holy to the Lord.')and to offer a sacrifice according to what is said in the Law of the Lord, a pair of turtledoves, or two young pigeons. Now there was a man in Jerusalem, whose name was Simeon, and this man was righteous and devout, **waiting for the consolation of Israel, and the Holy Spirit was upon Him.** And it had been revealed to him by the Holy Spirit that he would not see death before he had seen the Lord's Christ."*

What an amazing thing to be said. He was righteous. Devout. The Holy Spirit was upon him. He was watching for the promises of God to come true.

I think putting people in "super-spiritual status" categories can keep me from realizing that I can also watch for the Savior.

I may not be living my days in a temple. I may be busy trying to fit in yet another Christmas party, watch my nephew's Christmas play at school, bake my favorite Christmas cookies—but what if, in the middle of all this, I am watching for the Messiah in my life?

Watching for the promises of God to come true. Watching for the presence of God in the middle of my Monday.

Asking God to fill me with the Holy Spirit so that I can live out the fruits of the Spirit.

> *".. and when the parents brought in the child Jesus, to do for him according to the custom of the Law, he took him up in his arms and blessed God and said, 'Lord, now you are letting your servant depart in peace, according to your word;* **for my eyes have seen your salvation** *that you have prepared in the presence of all peoples, a light for revelation to the Gentiles, and for glory to your people Israel.'" (Luke 2:26-29)*

Simeon's eyes saw what he was watching for. He saw the light.

Find yourself a good strand of Christmas lights. Hopefully, your tree is not like mine, where one whole strand of lights is out because I cannot figure out which bulb burnt out.

Look at those lights. Now think about watching for the light of Christ in your life.

Look for the Savior.

Simeon was not the only one watching and waiting.

There was a prophetess named Anna. I love that title. Could you please refer to me as prophetess Jenn?

Sweet Anna was a widow. You will love talking to her at the Christmas party. I get the sense you will want to lean in close and hear her feeble voice speak of when she got to meet the One she had been waiting to meet.

I used to have a widowed neighbor named Zelda. She lived above me in my apartment complex, and she was always watching for me. She knew if I was having people over to eat. Pretty soon, I would find Zelda at my door asking if she could come in.

My favorite was the time she joined us for Thanksgiving. She didn't like to keep her teeth in, and my nieces had no concept of the idea of false teeth.

They were slightly traumatized when Zelda took her teeth out and placed them on the napkin right beside her pumpkin pie plate.

I am not sure the situation of prophetess Anna's teeth, but I know this—she was a watching worshiper.

"And there was a prophetess, Anna, the daughter of Phanuel, of the tribe of Asher. She was advanced in years, having lived with her husband seven years from when she was a virgin, and then as a widow until she was eighty-four. She did not depart from the temple, worshiping with fasting and prayer night and day. And coming up at that very hour she began to give thanks to God and to speak of him to all who were waiting for the redemption of Jerusalem."

Imagine the moment when she got to hold heaven on earth when she met Jesus at the temple that day. The one she had waited for she was able to worship.

I want to have a heart like Anna. I want to speak of my redemption story.

I want to remember that the greatest gift of Christmas is unwrappable.

The greatest gift is that God came wrapped in the form of a baby in swaddling clothes.

This changed everything.

Friends, let's go ahead and call ourselves in the "spiritual ones" category because we are going to be watching and worshiping the King who has come.

Week Two Reading Guide

Day 8: John 2:4-7

Day 9: John 6:34

Day 10: Ruth 1 and 2

Day 11: Ruth 3 and 4

Day 12: Luke 1:5-24

Day 13: Luke 2:22-34

Day 14: Lyke 2:34-37

What do I learn about God in these scriptures?

How does what I learned about God change me?

How am I experiencing the King who has come, God with us?

ADVENTING WEEK THREE
Wonder

*I*T'S TIME WE talk about the stars of this
Christmas party.
Well besides Jesus, of course.

Mary and Joseph. Mom and Pops.

Chosen by God to be the parents of the son of
God. CAN YOU EVEN IMAGINE?

I am not a parent, but I have lots of friends who
are parents. I think parents are all amazing. They
are keeping their humans alive. Fed. Teaching
them all the things.

Navigating parenting in today's world of social
media experts seems exhausting to me. To baby-led
wean or not to wean?

Co-sleeping or <u>Babywise?</u> Are they going to be
on a schedule?

Instagram-perfect pancake Saturdays.

To vaccinate or to not vaccinate? People have
all kinds of opinions about all of the things.

The reality is there is no real clear guidebook to
parenting.

(Besides the Bible, of course, just like Jesus is the star of Christmas. But let's be honest the Bible does not really have much to say about whether your child should taste sugar before they are one year old—and P.S.: If they are the fourth child, of course, they have had sugar long before their first birthday cake, as opposed to the first baby who probably has not even smelled refined sugar yet.)

My friends that are parents of any age child are my heroes. As I lean in and listen to their hearts, their fears, their frustrations—it often boils down to one big question.

Am I getting this right?

That can be true of not just parents. Of all of us.

Am I getting this thing called life right? Am I making the right decisions? Am I enough? Am I failing at this?

Even in the holiday season, we can ask ourselves, am I doing this holiday thing right? Will my too many extension cords plugged in to try to make that glorious Christmas lights display burn the house down?

Will I find the right gift for Great Aunt Myrtle?

Will I make the right memories? Will I love my people well? Will I miss out? Will I fail? Do I matter?

So many questions.

Can you imagine the questions Mary and Joseph had? Told they would-be parents of the Son of God?

Will we get this right? Will we make the right memories? Will we love Jesus well? Will we miss out?

Will we fail the SON OF GOD?

Imagine the weight of it all.

There are several definitions of the word wonder. Wonder as a noun: "A feeling of surprise mingled with admiration caused by something beautiful, unexpected, or unexplainable."

Wonder as a verb: "To feel doubt. To desire or be curious about something."

How did Mary and Joseph move from wonder the verb "to feel doubt" to wonder as a noun, "a feeling of admiration caused by something beautiful, unexpected or unexplainable"?

Let's take a peek at the moment when it all began to change for them. The moments where angels came and brought them their unexpected birth announcement.

"In the sixth month, the angel Gabriel was sent from God to a city of Galilee named Nazareth, to a virgin betrothed to a man whose name was Joseph of the house of David. And the virgin's name was Mary. And He came to her and said, 'Greetings, O favored one, the Lord is with you.' But she was greatly troubled at this. 'Do not be afraid, Mary, for you have found favor with God. And behold, you will conceive in your womb and bear a son, and you shall call his name Jesus. He will be great and will be called the Son of the Most High. ' and Mary said to the angel, 'how will this be since I am virgin?' And the angel answered her, 'The Holy Spirit will overshadow you; therefore, the child to be born will be called holy—the Son of God.'" (Luke 1:26-35)

I would have to pull Mary aside at the Christmas party and have her recount this story all over again.

I would want to know way more details.

Luke tells us she was greatly troubled by this news. **I believe that is an understatement.**

I would want to know how she felt about an angel showing up in her room. About the fact that she was going to have to defend her reputation in a world that was going to tell her she should be ashamed.

I know there had to be a great deal of doubt going through her mind. Like how could this be since I am a virgin?

If I were her, I would be thinking, "Should I tell Joseph about this in a text message because that feels a whole lot easier than a phone call?"

Or would there be a tiny part of me that wanted to go viral on social media by making a video telling everyone I was going to be the mother of the Son of God?

I am amazed at how Mary moved from wonder as a verb to wonder as a noun. Wonder as a noun turned to worship.

> *"And Mary said, 'Behold, I am the servant of the Lord; let it be according to your word.'" (Luke 1:38)*

Can we turn our doubt into a worship moment like this?

Can I open my hands and heart to Jesus and tell Him my fears? My questions? My "am I going to get this right? "

Can I whisper to Him, "This feels impossible" and hear Him whisper back, "For nothing will be impossible with God?" (Luke 1:27).

Can you open your hands and tell Him your fears?

Tell Him you are wondering if He picked the right one for the job. For the family. For this situation. For this calling. For these children. For this relationship. For this trial.

I believe we can celebrate together that as we run to Him with these questions, we can open our hearts to say, "Let it be according to your word."

I am staring at a plaque right on my bookshelf that my dear friend Deb Brown made for me. She wrote a wonderful book called *Brave as a Girl can Be: Let's Get off the Fear Cycle and Live Free* and gave me this plaque to celebrate the first Brave Girl conference we did together. (P.S.: You can grab a copy of her book on Amazon. You will not regret it!)

The plaque says, "He makes me brave," Isaiah 41:10.

> *"Fear Not for I am with You. Be not dismayed for I am your God; I will strengthen you, I will help you, I will uphold you with my righteous right hand."*

I remember when I first got her book, I was thinking to myself, "I do not need help being brave." For those of you that know me, you know

I live a pretty crazy life that takes me around the world into situations that can be pretty dangerous.

In her book, Deb describes asking herself what does fear look like in my life? She says on page 26, "The words came like a flurry. The faces of fear were not what I expected to see. As I sat back and looked intently at the list, I recognized myself in each one."

- Procrastination (Hello, let me add how long it has taken me to write this book.)
- Anger
- Perfectionism
- Laziness
- Safe
- Control
- Worry
- Hiding
- Settling
- Compromise
- Shame
- Regret
- Lonely
- Protection
- Anxiety
- Insecurity

When I read this list Deb had made, I saw several of these in me. So maybe I did need some help with brave.

I wonder what Mary would have placed on this list.

I imagine she had some possible anger. This was not her life plan. Some worry. How am I going to keep the Son of God alive?

For sure, some lonely, anxiety, and insecurity.

Deb says on page 28, "As I became more and more aware of the fear cycle and how much time I was spending there, I could see where the disobedience came from. It was me struggling to keep some parts of my life under my own control. When I was refusing to obey God, I was choosing to play it safe."

Mary had to move out of play-it-safe mode when she said, "Let it be according to your word."

Where are you in play-it-safe mode? Playing it safe for me can mean fearing rejection so much that I do not want to put myself out there. I do not want to write words (because writing for me feels like walking in a room naked).

I can play it safe in relationships. I can play it safe in saying yes when I should have said no because I do not want to disappoint anyone.

I do not want to play it safe. I want to place my yes on the table before the Lord.

I want my wondering to turn to the wonderment that God would choose me, that He would use me and that He is pleased with me.

He chooses you. He longs to use you. And He is dancing over you with delight.

> *"And Mary said, 'My soul magnifies the Lord, and my spirit rejoices in God my Savior, for he has looked on the humble estate of his servant. For behold, from now on all generations will call me blessed; for he who is mighty has done great things for me, and holy is his name. And his mercy is for those who fear him from generation to generation. He has shown strength with his arm, he has scattered the proud in the thoughts of their hearts; he had brought down the mighty from their thrones and exalted those of humble estate; he has filled the hungry with good things.'" (Luke 1:46-54)*

From wondering to wonder turned to worship. Let's join Mary this Christmas season.

And then there is Joseph

I feel like Joseph looks like quite the Hallmark-type prince charming star in this scenario.

Why is it that everything goes back to Hallmark movies for me? Sorry guys, if you happen to be reading this Advent study.

Can you imagine your fiancé telling you that she was pregnant with the Son of God from the Holy Spirit?

Let's get real here friends that seems like reality TV show stuff in the making.

Joseph has his angelic visitor appear to him in a dream.

> *"Joseph, son of David, do not fear to take Mary as your wife, for that which is conceived in her is from the Holy Spirit. She will bear a son, and you shall call his name Jesus for He will save his people from their sins."*

I wonder if Joseph asked the angel questions? I would have.

We may not know what questions Joseph asked, but we do know how He responded.

> *"When Joseph woke from sleep, he did as the angel of the Lord commanded him, he took his wife but knew her not until she had given birth to a son. And he called his name Jesus."*

I love how the Bible gives us some of the juicy details while keeping it rated G. He knew her not. Let's read between the lines about what that means.

(Unless you are doing this devotional with your kids and you can skip that last part.)

Joseph lived an obedient yes to the Lord. He took faith steps instead of getting stuck in fear stops.

He did not divorce her quietly as he first wanted.

He obeyed the Lord and said yes to being the father/non-father of Immanuel, God with us.

We will find after the birth of Jesus that Joseph took some more obedient yes steps. In Matthew 2, there is another angel with some more instructions for Joseph to follow.

> *"Now when they had departed,*
> *behold an angel of the Lord appeared*
> *to Joseph in a dream and said, 'Rise,*
> *to the child and his mother and flee*
> *to Egypt and remain there until I tell*
> *you, for Herod is about to search for*
> *the child to destroy Him.'" (Matthew*
> *2:13)*

This would not have been an easy journey. If I were Joseph and Mary, I would want to stay put. I would not want to journey into the foreign land of Egypt.

My fear steps might have become fear stops.

But Joseph led his family by listening to the voice of the Lord. God said, go, so he went.

It reminds me of the story of Abraham. Abraham is also told to go on a journey.

> *"Now the Lord said to Abram, 'Go*
> *from our country and your kindred*
> *and your father's house to the land*
> *that I will show you. '" (Genesis 12:1)*

Do you feel like me when you read that sentence? Like maybe God left some key details out?

The how? The what you will need for the journey. What you will encounter on the journey. The turn by turn directions GPS style.

Sometimes on my journey through this trying-to-live-out-my-faith life, I would like some more turn by turn directions, preferably in the Italian accent I set my GPS to tell me directions.

God said go to Abraham, and he went. "*So Abram went as the Lord had told him.*" *(Genesis 12:5)*

God said go to Joseph, and he went. First, he took Mary as his wife. Then he took her from Nazareth to Bethlehem, where Jesus would be born. Then we find him obediently following the instruction from the Lord to go to Egypt.

Sometimes you may feel like God is leaving out some details. Some turn by turn directions.

Let's be honest here—the unknown can scare us. It can leave room for us to make up lots of what could happen or what might happen ideas in our head.

And those usually are not the best-case scenarios that we make up in our minds and hearts.

It's not the best-case scenarios that are keeping us awake at night.

Train Maps

I will never forget my first time traveling overseas. I was appointed to serve as a summer missionary in the great big country of Japan.

It's a big family joke now because I was terrified to tell my parents that their girl who had never been on an airplane was going to spend the summer in a faraway land called Japan.

I told several folks before I got up the nerve to tell my parents.

That was where I got myself in trouble.

I forgot to tell those friends that I had not told my parents yet that I was going to Japan.

I bet you wish that you could have been in my driveway that day when a friend was dropping me back off at my house and started chatting with my mom.

She then asked my mom, "So how are you feeling about your daughter going to spend the summer in Japan?"

Oops! My mom tried to cover it up like she was well aware of my globetrotting plans. Let's say there may or may not have been a slightly heated discussion after my friend's mom pulled out of our driveway.

I loved my summer in Japan so much. I spent that summer in a wide-eyed wonder to a world that was very different from my own.

The train system, for example. Tennessee folk do not do much riding on trains—we find ourselves stopped in cars in front of railroad tracks as they cross.

In Japan, the train system is extensive. So many different lines of trains that take you anywhere you can imagine.

The train map was a tangled web of getting on this train and this line to get here, then transferring to go there. With my inability to read a map—amazingly, I am not still in Japan trying to find my way back to the house where I was staying.

I studied that train map. I memorized that train map. I road all around following that train map. And I sometimes found myself lost because I had read the train map wrong.

Here is a funny for you. When I got back from my summer in Japan, my church asked me to report on my trip. While I was on the stage, the pastor asked me if I wanted to pray in Japanese over the church.

As if I had learned fluent Japanese while I was there. I only knew how to ask for the bathroom, to say I was lost, and to tell someone that their food was good.

I was having a prideful moment on the stage that day, so I did not tell them I could not pray in Japanese.

I closed my eyes, and in the most eloquent way possible I prayed the names of all the train stations in the order that I had memorized them on the map. I also threw in the other sentence that I "knew." The train is approaching soon" sounds very fancy in Japanese.

I followed it up with a hearty "amen," and the people were so impressed.

Except for my Japanese friend that I forgot I had invited to church. He was very confused about why I kept telling the congregation that the train was approaching soon!

Those train maps were my direction source. Even when it seemed to be a tangled web that did not make sense, I followed.

And when I got it wrong, I would study the map again and try to get back on the right path.

> *Trust in the Lord with all your heart, and do not lean on your own understanding. In all your ways, acknowledge him, and he will make straight your paths." (Proverbs 3:5-6)*

I imagine there were many points on this journey of being the "father/not father" of Jesus that Joseph felt lost. He wondered how this path would be made straight. How was this story going to end? Would it make sense along the way?

There are many points on our faith journey when we may feel the same way. How is this story going to end? Will I get lost along the way? Am I going to end up where I need to be?

Matthew 1:22 tells us that all this took place to fulfill what the Lord had spoken by the prophet.

We hear that again in Matthew 2:15 when Joseph was told to take Mary and Jesus to Egypt. *"This was to fulfill what was spoken by the prophet, 'Out of Egypt I called My Son.'"*

After some time in Egypt, an angel appears again to tell Joseph that it is time to return to Nazareth.

*"And being warned in a dream, he withdrew to the district of Galilee. And he went and lived in a city called Nazareth, that **what was spoken by the prophets might be fulfilled.**"*

God was granting his direction because He knew the way. He knew the plan. He knew the details.

We may not be having angelic visitors telling us where to go next, but we do have the guidance of the Holy Spirit and the Bible's guiding words.

Friend, where do you need direction? Where do you sense God is calling you to journey? To walk? To take obedient faith steps?

Where are those steps becoming fear stops?

Can we trust that the same God who details this story is detailing our stories for His glory?

I believe that we can.

I *know* that we can.

And I know that on the days when we are afraid we can't, we can run to the One who is guiding us and tell Him that.

I am afraid. I need peace. I need direction. I need clarity.

> *"If anyone lacks wisdom, let him ask God, who gives generously to all without reproach, and it will be given him." (James 1:5)*

Week Three Reading Guide

Day 15: Luke 1:26-38

Day 16: Luke 1:39-53

Day 17: Isaiah 43

Day 18 Matthew 1: 18-25

Day 19: Matthew 2:13-23

Day 20: Genesis 12

Day 21: Luke 2:1-7

What do I learn about God in these scriptures?

How does what I learned about God change me?

How am I experiencing the King who has come, God with us?

ADVENTING WEEK FOUR
Worship

D O YOU FEEL like you are skating on into the end of this advent season on a wing and a prayer? Maybe I am saying that because that is how I feel coming to the end of writing this book.

My reward for finishing these words is that today my sister and her kiddos are coming over to put my Christmas tree and ornaments up. Sure, it's still a few weeks before Thanksgiving, but I have been deep in this Advent thing, so I am ready to celebrate.

I am celebrating with you today. We have taken time this season to wait on the coming King.

To watch for the coming King.

To wonder at how the God who detailed the Christmas story is detailing our lives.

Every week is leading up to the fact that we get to worship. Worship the King who has come.

"In those days, a decree went out from Caesar Augustus that all the world should be registered. This was the first registration when Quirinius was governor of Syria. And all went to be registered, each to his own town. And Joseph also went up from Galilee, from the town of Nazareth, to Judea, to the City of David, which is called Bethlehem, because he was of the house and lineage of David, to be registered with Mary, his betrothed, who was with child. And while they were there, the time came for her to give birth. And she gave birth to her firstborn son and wrapped him in swaddling cloths and laid him in a manger because there was no place for them in the inn." (Luke 2:1-7)

Here it is friend. This is the point in a musical score where the crescendo happens. Where all that is building reaches the height. (I am trying to pretend like I know things here about music. I am not sure I even used the right words there. So forgive me choir and piano teacher of years gone by if I did not.)

The time for heaven to burst forth to earth.

I have been to Bethlehem. It is incredible to be in the town where the birth of one baby boy changed everything!

I was so excited to be there. In my Bible above Luke 2, I have written Bethlehem 2016, 2017, 2018. I wanted to remember what it felt like to read those words while I was there—in that very place.

They have built an orthodox church to protect the place where they believe Jesus was born.

They may not be 100 percent sure if this is the exact place the stable would have been where Jesus was born, but in my heart and mind it is closer than any fake nativity we have here in Tennessee, so I am going to enjoy the sacredness of the moment of at least being in the vicinity of where that holy birth moment could have occurred.

In case you didn't know, stables were not the fancy barns that are so popular today. You have seen the trend. Barns that are so beautiful there is no way an animal has ever eaten, or let's be honest here, pooped in them.

Barns that people pay the big bucks to host their wedding or party.

This was not the stable where the God of the universe was born. The stables of that day were more like caves.

Caves where animals did eat and sleep and poop.

I was filled with emotions as I stood in line to visit the place where Jesus could have been born.

It's very interesting. To get into the scene of the nativity, you have to duck down low.

You also have to be quiet. The priests that guard this place are very serious about this.

I may or may not have almost gotten kicked out of the line because quiet is not always the easiest for me, and I have a hard time holding in laughter when I am not supposed to laugh.

I found it so significant that you have to bend down low to enter. If you try to go inside the door of the nativity standing high, you cannot enter.

What a beautiful picture of how Jesus came. He humbled Himself. He bends down low to get us. He rescues us because He delights in us.

He rescues you because He delights in you.

> *"He sent from on high, he took me, he drew me out of many waters. He rescued me from my strong enemy and from those who hated me, for they were too mighty for me. They confronted me in the day of my calamity, but the Lord was my support. He brought me out into a broad place. He rescued me because He delighted in me." (Psalm 18:16-19)*

"Have this mind among yourselves, which is yours in Christ Jesus, who though he was in the form of God, did not count equality with God a thing to be grasped, but made himself nothing, taking the form of a servant, being born in the likeness of men. And being found in human form, he humbled himself by becoming obedient to the point of death, even death on a cross. Therefore God has highly exalted him and bestowed on him the name that is above every name, so that at the name of Jesus every knee should bow, in heaven and on earth and under the earth, and every tongue confess that Jesus Christ is Lord, to the glory of God the Father." (Philippians 2:5-11)

He was brought low so that we could reach Him.

I can hardly wrap my mind around it.

As much as I loved getting to visit the place where they believe Jesus could have been born, honestly, it was the shepherds' field that captured my heart.

You find it tucked away from the hustle and bustle. It's a little known spot that most groups do not go to—so I am not going to tell you where it is. (Like I could give you any details of how to get anywhere in Israel. Remember, I cannot find my way around my home town.)

There is another cave there where animals would have gone. There is a field where the shepherds could have been watching their flock by night.

The thing that captured my heart was the manger in this field.

When you see a manger in our current nativity scenes, generally it is constructed out of wood. It has a nice bed of hay, and it looks like a very rustic version of a crib.

In all reality, mangers did not look like that.

The rough stone was chiseled hard, formed into a manger.

Something happened in my heart when I saw that stone manger in the shepherds' field.

I put my actual Bible in the manger and took a picture. This is what I wrote on Instagram:

> *"I think this was my favorite picture that I took in Israel. The whole time in Israel, walking the streets where the stories happened from Genesis to the New Testament, I was reminded of this, that the Word became flesh and lived among us. The mighty fit in a manger."*

The mighty God made Himself fit in a manger.

This caused the shepherds to worship in a field one day. It brought me to my knees while I was in Israel that day.

This reminder can cause us to pause and worship the King who has come today.

In the Field

Shepherds were not the most beloved folks in the bunch. After all, they hung outside with dirty, smelly sheep.

We probably have all been to a petting zoo at some point in our life. I can picture the smell right now. The mixture of stink trying to be covered up by fresh wood chips. You cannot leave that petting zoo without the lingering reminder that you visited it.

Every time I go to a petting zoo, the goats try to eat some article of my clothing. Maybe it's because they somehow know that I owned goats at one time when I was in Nepal, and those goats may or may not have been eaten in the church potluck one day.

I love that God chose to send His angels to come to the stinky shepherds who were busy tending sheep.

"And in the same region there were shepherds out in the field, keeping watch over their flock by night. And an angel of the Lord appeared to them, and the glory of the Lord shone around them, and they were filled with fear. And the angel said to them, 'Fear not, for behold, I bring you good news of a great joy that will be for all the people. For unto you is born this day in the city of David, a Savior who is Christ the Lord. And this will be a sign to you; you will find a baby wrapped in swaddling cloths and laying in a manger.' And suddenly there was with the angel a multitude of the heavenly host praising God and saying, 'Glory to God in the highest, and on earth peace among those with who he is pleased.'" (Luke 2:9-15)

The angels quickly turned the mundane moment of watching the sheep into majesty.

Have you seen those flash music mobs that occasionally take the internet by storm? I am fascinated by them.

I am thinking of one I saw in the mall here in my hometown. One brave soul steps out and begins to sing the first few lines of a song.

Can you imagine being that first brave one to sing the first song?

Then, before you know it, people all around are stepping out of the shadows, joining in the song.

In this scene, an angel stepped out and declared some good news.

Some REALLY good news. News that would bring joy for all of the people.

The news was so good other angels joined in. A multitude of heavenly hosts.

This Christmas season really should be about celebrating this REALLY good news. News that is for all people.

There is so much bad news in our world today.

It can get overwhelming. It can be easy to become overwhelmed by all the negative. To be stuck in our bad news.

What if we paused right now and listen to that first angel calling out a reminder to us today?

Fear Not.
I have brought you good news of
great joy that is FOR YOU.

The King has come.

And then join our hearts with the multitude of angels proclaiming glory to God in the highest.

Just a note, I am not recommending that you have to go and start your flash mob to do this. That is, unless you want to.

I am recommending that we all pause in the middle of our normal. In the middle of the Christmas rush and turn our hearts to worship because the King has come.

Bring Your Gifts

Today is the day of the essential oil craze. I am not going to lie. I like me some good essential oils, so I am not knocking my essential oil selling sisters and brothers.

But I do think they are bringing frankincense back. It was not a thing many people knew about before our oily friends.

Neither was kombucha. I feel like both are living in their hay day right now.

What I did know about frankincense was that the wisemen brought some to Jesus.

The wisemen were looking for Jesus to worship Him. To lay their gifts before Him.

I love this about them. They were serious about finding Jesus.

I got so tickled about my sister on her Instagram stories last week. Her loud and crazy and full of fun family of six were decorating for Christmas. They were looking everywhere for the baby Jesus that went in the nativity.

And let me add that this nativity was a mixture of a bunch of different nativity scenes that all seemed to be missing pieces from the years, so they just put them all together.

A few were clay figures made in Peru, a few handmade from straw in Nepal, and the Veggie Tales nativity scene all mixed.

The only thing missing?

Jesus.

They couldn't find Him in any of their nativity scenes.

You could see them running around in the video trying to find Jesus.

They finally did find one Jesus who looked more like a grown man rolled up in tissue paper than a baby in swaddling clothes. Not sure what happened there.

I feel like that sometimes. That if people were watching a video of my life it would look like I am running around searching trying to find Jesus because I feel like He has gone missing in my life.

The truth is, He never leaves me.

He never leaves you.

Sometimes we might lose track of him because we stop looking for Him.

It seems fitting that we call the men looking for Jesus the **wise**men. They were looking for Him to worship Him. To bring their gifts to offer Him.

"When they saw the star, they rejoiced exceedingly with great joy! And going into the house they saw the child with Mary his mother, and they fell down and worshipped him. Then, opening their treasures, they offered him gifts, gold and frankincense and myrrh." (Matthew 2:7-11)

They found Him. They worshipped Him. They offered gifts to Him.

Since this is the last week of Advent, this should be around present opening time. The time when you gather together with each other and gift things.

Picture yourself as one of the wisemen. You have been looking for Jesus this season. You have been on a journey of faith. You have followed your version of the star.

And you have found Him.

What do you want to offer Him? What gifts of your heart do you want to lay before him?

You have waited. You have watched. You have wondered. Now, it is time to worship.

Father, I pray for my friend who has taken this Advent journey. I pray as she/he opens gifts this season that she/he receives the gift of knowing You in a new way. In a deeper way.

I pray that she/he continues to hope for you in the barren places.

I pray for my friend that you will meet he/him in his/her doubts. His or Her fears. His or Her wondering if she/he is doing it right.

Jesus, thank You that You are the Promise Keeper. That you came just as You said You would. We worship You—the King who HAS come and who is coming again.

You are faithful. You are the star of Christmas. Jesus, forgive us when we lose sight of You. When we stop looking for You.

Jesus help us to wait for You. To watch for You. To be in awe and wonder of You. And to worship You.

In Jesus' name,
Amen.

Week Four Reading Guide

Day 22: Luke 2:8-14

Day 23: Luke 2:15-21

Day 24: Matthew 2:1-12

Day 25 Reread Luke 1, 2

Matthew 1, Matthew 2

What do I learn about God in these scriptures?

How does what I learned about God change me?

How am I experiencing the King who has come, God with us?

Let's Be Friends

THE ADVENT STUDY is over, but can we still be friends?

I love keeping up with you. I wish I could have you over to my house for coffee and a dinner party.

But since I live in a one-bedroom apartment and I cannot fit you all, can I invite you to visit me in my internet home?

Would love to have you at www.comingalive-ministries.com

You can go by there and sign up to get fun random occasional e-mail newsletters from me (I promise I will not spam you).

You can keep up with my podcast, Coming Alive Conversations. This is one of my favorite things. I get to interview amazing people that I LOVE sharing with you. You can listen on my website or you can search Coming Alive Conversations and subscribe for FREE on your favorite podcast app.

A new episode releases every Monday.

Feel free to friend me on the socials.

@comingaliveJenn on Instagram and Twitter

Jenn@ Coming Alive Ministries on Facebook

Feel free to e-mail me anytime and let me know how I can be praying for you.

And can I sheepishly ask you to leave a review for this book on Amazon (and don't forget my biggest fear is rejection so try to be nice)

I love coming alive with you friends.

Blessings

Jenn Hand

Special Thanks

I COULDN'T WRITE this book without adding a special thanks page.

First special thanks: Casey Bagley, my wonderful friend who has signed up to be my editor of all of my books. I do not think she knew what this would entail (especially with all my long adjectives). Casey I am so beyond proud of you—victory sister. These words could not happen without your gift, and I am so thankful. Let's have coffee and bacon!

I am an enneagram 7. An extrovert. I need ALL the people. So I could not stick it out and write a book without some amazing people.

Thanks to my amazing sister who helped me refine this idea. Michelle I am so grateful for your constant cheering and for the amazing example of servanthood you are.

My parents: You probably didn't even know I was writing this book because I am hard to keep up with, but I am so beyond blessed to be your daughter. Thanks for always believing in my ministry and being a huge part of coming alive.

The Coming Alive Board: You are not just the "board' you are my dearest friends. Thanks so much for all that you do. Casey and Barry Lewis, JP and Catrina Pruitt, Justin and Brittany Smith, Michelle, and Todd Humbert, Houston Gibson. Thanks for going on this crazy faith journey with me.

Deb Brown—you are my Bravest friend, and our daily texts and being God-sized dream sisters is the BEST gift.

Tina Barringer—Who would have thought that I would have found the dearest friend I didn't know I was missing through teacher training! What a gift. I love our daily phone calls and shenanigans. You constantly inspire me, and I am so thankful for you

The Tuesday night girls: Thanks for being my favorite safest place of community. I love coming alive with you each week, and I thought of you the whole time I was writing this

And thanks to my Wednesday night small group friends. Thanks for letting me join your group, and for the ways being in your group has been such a fun gift of laughter and growth.

Made in the USA
Monee, IL
14 December 2020